AF207669

MOHAWK

Big Buddy Books
An Imprint of Abdo Publishing
abdopublishing.com

Katie Lajiness

abdopublishing.com

Published by Abdo Publishing, a division of ABDO, PO Box 398166, Minneapolis, Minnesota 55439.
Copyright © 2019 by Abdo Consulting Group, Inc. International copyrights reserved in all countries. No part
of this book may be reproduced in any form without written permission from the publisher. Big Buddy Books™
is a trademark and logo of Abdo Publishing.

Printed in the United States of America, North Mankato, Minnesota.
052018
092018

THIS BOOK CONTAINS
RECYCLED MATERIALS

Cover Photo: Xinhua/Alamy Stock Photo.
Background Photo: Katie Dobies/Getty Images.
Interior Photos: Chronicle/Alamy Stock Photo (p. 30); Getty Images (p. 26); Jack Unruh/National Geographic Creative
    (p. 21); Jupiterimages/Getty Images (p. 19); Ken Wiedemann/Getty Images (p. 25); Lawrence Manning/Getty
    Images (p. 27); Marilyn Angel Wynn/Getty Images (p. 15); Marilyn Angel Wynn/Native Stock (pp. 9, 16, 17);
    Megapress/Alamy Stock Photo (p. 29); North Wind Picture Archives (p. 23); Philippe Demande/Getty Images
    (p. 11); Ryan Remiorz/AP Images (p. 5); tatianatatiana/Getty Images (p. 13).

Coordinating Series Editor: Tamara L. Britton
Contributing Editor: Jill Roesler
Graphic Design: Jenny Christensen, Maria Hosley

Library of Congress Control Number: 2017962683

Publisher's Cataloging-in-Publication Data

Name: Lajiness, Katie, author.
Title: Mohawk / by Katie Lajiness.
Description: Minneapolis, Minnesota : Abdo Publishing, 2019. | Series: Native Americans
    set 4 | Includes online resources and index.
Identifiers: ISBN 9781532115097 (lib.bdg.) | ISBN 9781532155819 (ebook)
Subjects: LCSH: Mohawk Indians--Juvenile literature. | Indians of North America--
    Juvenile literature. | Indigenous peoples--Social life and customs--Juvenile literature.
    | Cultural anthropology--Juvenile literature.
Classification: DDC 970.00497--dc23

CONTENTS

AMAZING PEOPLE

Hundreds of years ago, North America was mostly wild, open land. Native American tribes lived on the land. Each had its own language and **customs**.

The Mohawk (MOH-hawk) are one Native American tribe. Many know them for their **ceremonies** and handmade crafts. Let's learn more about these Native Americans.

Did You Know?

The Mohawk call themselves *Kahniakehake*, which means "people of the land of gun flint."

The Mohawk are one of the first five tribes in the League of the Iroquois.

MOHAWK TERRITORY

Today there are 562 Native American tribes in the US. And there are 617 **indigenous** communities in Canada. The Mohawk are just one of those tribes.

In the United States, Mohawk homelands are near the Hudson and Saint Lawrence rivers in New York and Vermont. They are also in Ontario and Quebec in Canada.

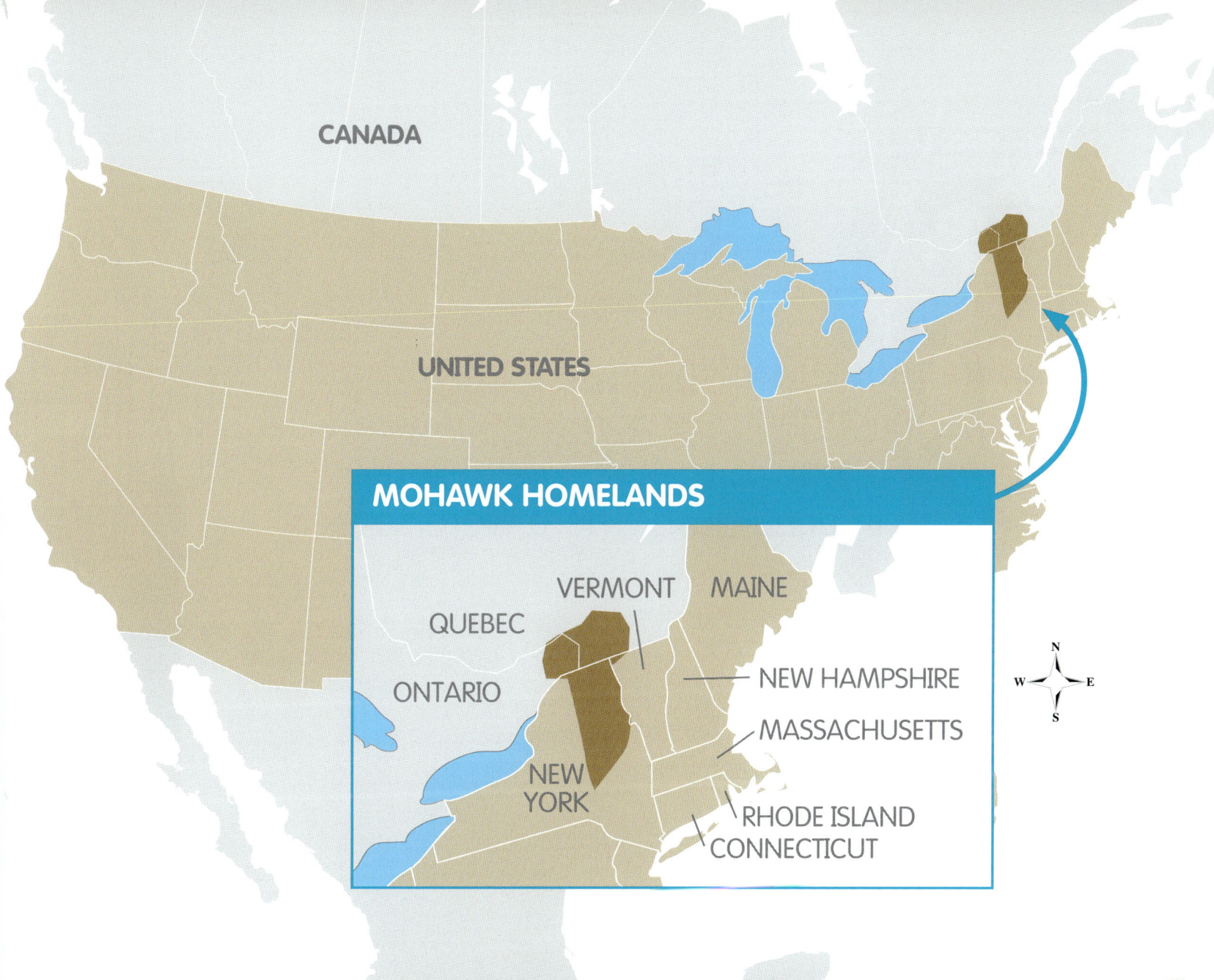

CANADA

UNITED STATES

MOHAWK HOMELANDS

VERMONT   MAINE

QUEBEC

ONTARIO   NEW HAMPSHIRE

                          MASSACHUSETTS

NEW
YORK
                          RHODE ISLAND
                          CONNECTICUT

N
W · E
S

MEXICO

HOME LIFE

Mohawk people lived in large, bark-covered houses called longhouses. Some longhouses were up to 200 feet (61 m) long! Many families lived together in one house. There were several longhouses in each village.

Longhouses sat next to small farms. Forests and bodies of water covered much of the surrounding land.

What They Ate

The Mohawks mostly ate their own crops. Women grew corn, beans, and squash. But they also ate bear and deer meat. Sometimes, they would fish. They also gathered nuts and berries.

The Mohawk hunted deer with a bow and arrows.

Daily Life

Mohawks wore clothes made from deerskin. They used porcupine quills and beads to decorate their moccasins. Women wore dresses and shawls. Men wore loincloths and leggings.

Mohawks sometimes wore their hair smooth on both sides of their heads. But they left a strip of spiked hair or feathers running down the center.

13

Men and women had different jobs. Men hunted and fished for food. They often traveled on horseback. This way, men could carry heavy animals back to the village.

Women farmed the land and gathered food in the forest. They also took care of the longhouses and raised the children. Women always governed the Mohawk tribes.

Tribes called corn, beans, and squash the Three Sisters. That is because women usually planted these crops together.

MADE BY HAND

The Mohawk made many objects by hand. They often used natural supplies. These arts and crafts added beauty to everyday life.

Beaded Moccasins
Women sewed beads onto moccasins to make them look beautiful.

Snowshoes

Snowshoes had wooden frames and leather webbing. They helped men walk on top of deep snow while hunting.

Water Drum with Stick

Tribes used a wood base and animal hides to make a drum. Then, they poured water inside to make a new sound.

Double Ball Game

Women sewed deerskin balls to play a game that is like lacrosse.

Spirit Life

To give thanks to their Creator, the Mohawk danced and sang songs. Then they listened to the Thanksgiving Address. Through this address, the Mohawk people learned how their tribe connects to all living things.

The Mohawk were one of the first tribes to play lacrosse. They believed the game was a gift from their Creator.

STORYTELLERS

Stories are important to the Mohawk. Mohawks respect all living things. For centuries, children have learned about the tribe through storytelling. Older tribe members tell about the sun, wind, stars, and animal spirits.

Mohawk storytellers used items such as feathers to help tell stories.

FIGHTING FOR LAND

Long ago, the Mohawk people lived peaceful lives. In the 1500s, the Mohawk met the Spanish settlers. The British, Dutch, and French followed. During the **French and Indian War**, the Mohawk fought for the British.

The **American Revolution** separated the Mohawk people into two groups. Some fought for the British and some fought for the Americans. Afterward, Europeans continued to settle on tribal lands. By the mid-1800s, the US government forced the Mohawk people to live on **reservations**.

After living with Europeans, some Mohawks caught new illnesses such as smallpox and measles. About half of all Native Americans died.

23

For hundreds of years, the US government controlled the Mohawk tribe. They were not allowed to practice their beliefs or **customs** until the mid-1900s.

But Native Americans continued to fight for their land. In 1989, the Mohawk objected when their land became a golf course. Sadly, the tribe members did not get their land back.

The Bridge of Flowers is part of the Mahican-Mohawk Trail. This was a 100-mile (161 m) trail used by Mohawk tribe members.

BACK IN TIME

1534

The Mohawks first met the French.

1613

Mohawks signed their first **treaty** with Dutch settlers.

1710

Chiefs of the three Mohawk bands visited Queen Anne of England.

1783

The Treaty of Paris set the border between Canada and the United States. This treaty separated Mohawk land into two parts.

1812

The United States and Britain fought a battle on Mohawk lands.

1988

Mohawk Chief Jake Swamp planted a tree during a **ceremony** in Washington, DC. It still stands near the Lincoln and Vietnam Veterans memorials.

2003

The Mohawk settled a land deal with the Canadian government. The tribe received payment and 8,300 acres (3,300 ha) of land.

2017

The Mohawk tribe created a technology center. They wanted to continue educating the Mohawk in science, technology, and math.

The Mohawk Today

The Mohawk have a long, rich history. Many remember them for bravely fighting their enemies. Mohawk roots run deep. Today, the people have held on to those special things that make them Mohawk. Even though times have changed, many people carry the **traditions**, stories, and memories of the past into the present.

Did You Know?

As of 2012, more than 25,000 Mohawks lived in the US and Canada.

Mohawks gathered at the 2017 Kahnawake Powwow in Ontario, Canada. There, they danced and practiced their customs.

"What is past is past —
it is the present and the
future that concern us."

— Hiawatha, Mohawk

GLOSSARY

American Revolution the war between Americans and the British from 1775 to 1783.

ceremony a formal event on a special occasion.

custom a practice that has been around a long time and is common to a group or a place.

French and Indian War the war between France and Great Britain from 1754 to 1763.

indigenous produced, living, or existing naturally in a particular region or environment.

reservation (reh-zuhr-VAY-shuhn) a piece of land set aside by the government for Native Americans to live on.

tradition (truh-DIH-shuhn) a belief, a custom, or a story handed down from older people to younger people.

treaty an agreement made between two or more groups.

Online Resources

Booklinks
NONFICTION NETWORK
FREE! ONLINE NONFICTION RESOURCES

To learn more about the Mohawk, visit **abdobooklinks.com**. These links are routinely monitored and updated to provide the most current information available.

INDEX